FUNDAMENTAL
KARATE

AIDAN TRIMBLE AND
DAVE HAZARD

First published 1993
Reprinted 1994

3 5 7 9 10 8 6 4

First published in the United Kingdom in 1993 by
Stanley Paul Limited,
Random House, 20 Vauxhall Bridge Road,
London SW1V 2SA

Random House Australia (Pty) Limited
20 Alfred Street, Milsons Point, Sydney, New South Wales 2061,
Australia

Random House New Zealand Limited
18 Poland Road, Glenfield, Auckland 10, New Zealand

Random House, South Africa (Pty) Limited
PO Box 337, Bergvlei, South Africa

Random House UK Limited Reg. No. 954009

A catalogue record for this book is available from
the British Library

ISBN 0 09 177545 0

Set in Rockwell by SX Composing Ltd, Rayleigh, Essex

Printed and bound in Great Britain by Butler & Tanner Ltd,
Frome, Somerset

Dave:
Audrey, Ben, Janice and Tracey for their love and support
Aidan:
To my son Maxwell

Contact address for authors:

PO Box 47,
West PDO,
Nottingham,
NG8 2EA,
England.

Acknowledgements

The authors gratefully acknowledge the following:

Richard LaPlante
Janice Hazard
Chris Hallam
Noel McCarthy
Roddy Bloomfield
Dominique Shead
Marion Paull
Ian MacLaren

Contents

Foreword by Richard LaPlante   **5**
Introduction: Right – from the start   **7**

1   **A Brief History of Shotokan Karate**   **8**
2   **Breathing – the essence of Karate**   **11**
    Kimé   12
    Kiai   14
3   **Use of the Hips (Koshi)**   **17**
4   **Stances (Dachi)**   **21**
    Zenkutsu-Dachi   22
    Kokutsu-Dachi   26
    Kiba-Dachi   30
5   **Punching (Tsuki)**   **33**
    Choku-Zuki   36
    Gyaku-Zuki   38
    Oi-Zuki   40
    Kizami-Zuki   42
6   **Blocking (Uke)**   **45**
    Age-Uke   46
    Soto-Uke   48
    Uchi-Uke   50
    Shuto-Uke   52
    Gedan-barai   54
7   **Kicking (Keri)**   **57**
    Mae-Geri   58
    Yoko-Geri-Keage   60
    Yoko-Geri-Kekomi   62
    Mawashi-Geri   66
    Ushiro-Geri   68
8   **Striking (Uchi)**   **71**
    Shuto-Uchi   72
    Nukite-Uchi   72
    Uraken-Uchi   76
    Empi-Uchi   78

Muscle System   79
Vulnerable Points of the Body   79
Glossary   80

Foreword

Richard LaPlante was born in Pennsylvania USA in 1948. He is a 3rd Dan JKA black belt in Karate, a qualified boxing coach, a psychiatric counsellor and a successful author. He now lives in Surrey, England.

The year was 1966 and *The Green Hornet*, featuring Bruce Lee, was the most popular series on American television. I was 18 years old and home from college on my summer break.

I never missed an episode of the series, waiting impatiently through plot and dialogue for the action sequences, when Kato, Lee's character, dispatched villains with kicks and punches like a scythe cutting grass.

He was a little guy, 5½ ft tall and only 130 lb – 9 st 4 lb – but he moved like a bolt of lightning.

Bruce Lee was the high point of my summer.

I wanted to be Bruce Lee.

'What was he doing? Kung Fu, Karate?' They were all the same to me, except there was no listing for 'Kung Fu' in my phone directory. There was, however, a Philadelphia Karate Club.

This was deep in the heart of West Philadelphia, the meanest streets my suburban, middle class feet had ever walked.

The *dojo* (training hall) was a converted supermarket with monsters inside – Japanese monsters, barking orders in their native tongue, demonstrating killer kicks and lethal punches, while controlling a group of men, each of whom I would have walked on the other side of the street to avoid.

A combination of curiosity laced with adrenaline overcame my fear; I pushed open the glass fronted doors and enrolled as a member, and then spent the remainder of the summer finding out the reality behind my television screen.

The 'monsters' were, in fact, some of the finest *'sensei'*, or teachers that the Japan Karate Association had ever produced: Teruyuki Okazaki, Kitura Kisaka and Keinosuke Enoeda, all in that converted supermarket, in West Philadelphia, instructing a single class.

The year 1966 seems a lifetime ago. Values have changed, styles have changed; I have grown up, married, and moved countries – from the United States to Great Britain.

Even Karate has changed – not in its traditional technique or discipline, but in the new order of *sensei* who have developed and emerged from *dojos* like that first one I attended in Philadelphia.

Teruyuki Okazaki and Keinosuke Enoeda, among other fine teachers, were the spiritual children of Shotokan Karate's founder, Gichin Funakoshi. They were ambassadors of their culture and art.

In that same way, Dave Hazard and Aidan Trimble form part of the legacy of our generation, Caucasians who have mastered the teachings of their Japanese *sensei* by devoting their lives to guiding others in the 'way of the empty hand'.

Fundamental Karate is part of their contribution to an art that has transcended time, language and culture. Learn from this book, and use it as a reference, as an inspiration.

And believe whatever you give to Karate, whether it is 10 months or 20 years, will be returned to you many times and will remain with you forever, enriching your life with the priceless gift of self-knowledge.

Trust Sensei Hazard and Sensei Trimble; they 'know'.

Richard LaPlante

INTRODUCTION
Right – From the Start

Many people stop practising Karate due to injury caused simply by performing techniques incorrectly. The self-inflicted misery of damaged knees, ankles or hip and elbow joints, lower back problems, strains, torn ligaments and hamstrings causes more agonies than the severest opponent. It is a strange irony when students who expect this martial art to make them fitter, healthier, more able to defend themselves, end up victims of their own misguided efforts.

An effective warm-up must precede all training. Follow this with the practice of the fundamental movements shown on the following pages and the possibility of injury should be minimised enabling you to progress quickly.

We cannot over-emphasise that however well produced a training guide may be and however ardently its rules are followed, it is no substitute for a good Karate School. Using this book to assist *dojo* (Karate Club) training can advance your development and hopefully enhance your enjoyment.

Select your Karate Club and instructor with great care. Don't make the mistake of joining the first club you visit, or the nearest one to home or the cheapest; similarly the most expensive does not necessarily mean the best. Choose with caution; it's important to make the right decision, as disappointment, even injury, at an early stage can be damaging to mind and body. It is worth spending time on research before making your commitment.

Karate practised properly is for all, and for all of your life.

Our best wishes to you for good health, enjoyment and a trouble free journey along the rewarding road to self-improvement.

Dave Hazard
Aidan Trimble

A BRIEF HISTORY OF SHOTOKAN KARATE

I.S. MACLAREN, 4TH DAN JKA

Shotokan karate is one of the most powerful and dynamic of the Japanese karate schools. By far the most widely practised style, it remains firmly rooted in its original martial arts tradition. It is the most comprehensive, both in the range of its techniques and the number and diversity of its Kata. To understand the basis of Shotokan, and to see the rich pedigree of its Kata and techniques, we need to look to its origins.

The first definite evidence of unarmed fighting methods appears on hieroglyphics on the tomb of Pharaoh Menes, the warrior king who first unified Egypt and who died around 3,000 BC. These pictures are of army training methods and show an unarmed combat technique which karateka would recognize as jodan uke in shiko dachi (a block to the face area, warrior in square stance). The Chinese emperor Shi-Huang-Di (221-206 BC) was buried at Xian with an army of some 7,000 life-size figures of horses and soldiers to guard him in the afterlife, and of particular interest are the figures of the officers, all unarmed and in postures showing they used a fighting method remarkably similar to karate. Throughout this period and after, the Chinese countryside was rife with bandits, and merchants hired bodyguards to protect their caravans. This eventually led to the development of the professional warrior, and it was under practical fighting conditions such as these that the martial arts evolved in the East.

The Ryukyu Islands, known to us as Okinawa, played a prominent role in karate's history. Formerly an independent kingdom, the Ryukyu became a Chinese vassal state in 1372. When the king, in an attempt to control the activities of local warlords, confiscated all weapons in 1429, there was a tremendous development of empty-hand fighting. In 1609 the islands were invaded by Japan and all weapons and martial arts were again banned; this again ensured the art's development to a formidable degree of efficiency. Most karate history has come down to us by word of mouth, and there are many tales of the great Okinawan karateka. Early historians believed that karate was developed by the peasants and traders to protect themselves, but more recent and detailed research has shown that it was in fact developed by the Okinawan military class (the Shizoku), and most of the great practitioners were members of the Okinawan Royal Guard. The term karate first appeared in general use in 1772, when Master Kanga (Tode) Sakugawa started to teach what he called Karate-no-Sakugawa. Sakugawa was a senior officer in the Palace Guard, and he was nicknamed 'Tode' (Karate) Sakugawa because of his proficiency in empty-hand fighting.

Shotokan is a modern name given to the style of karate that developed from the Okinawan Kobayashi Shorin Ryu School, and which was introduced to Japan in 1922 by Gichin Funakoshi, the 'father of modern karate'. He was born in 1868, and studied karate from his childhood. His teachers included such famous karate exponents as Master Sokon Matsumura, Commander of the Royal Palace Guard, Master Yatasune Azato and Master Yatasune Itosu.

Funakoshi first arrived in Japan in 1922, invited by the Japanese Ministry of Education to attend an athletic exhibition. His demonstration of karate was a great success, and while he remained unknown for a few more years, he was befriended by the founder of judo, Jigoro Kano, who invited him to teach at the Kodokan. Kano's help made a great impression on him, and he never forgot his kindness. The respect and courtesy he was shown probably influenced his own teaching and philosophy. Funakoshi was also befriended by the great Kendo master, Hiromichi Nakayama, who allowed him the use of his Dojo, and from whose teaching Funakoshi took the

elements of Tai Sabaki that we now use in Shotokan karate.

Between 1926 and 1930, Funakoshi developed karate further and consolidated its position in Japan. The Universities were the main sites of karate study, and they were influenced by Western research on physiology and calisthenics. During this period Funakoshi and his son Yoshitaka along with senior students Shigeru Egami, Isao Obata and Masatoshi Nakayama added kumite (fighting) methods, the Japanese kyu/dan ranking system, and some of the traditional concepts of budo (martial way) to the system. Under this group, the development of Shotokan karate really accelerated. The stances were studied and strengthened by being made lower so as to apply dynamic controlled stress to the leg muscles, and the effect of hip rotation on punches and kicks was also examined. This resulted in an increase in the power of punching and kicking techniques. This knowledge was incorporated into the kihon (basics) of Shotokan karate. After 1936, the Kata (sequences of movements) were revised to conform to the dynamic new style and several Kata from other styles were added to complete the system.

The word 'Shotokan' was chosen by Funakoshi's students to name his first personal dojo, and it derives from his pen name, 'Shoto', meaning 'pine wave', and 'kan', meaning hall. It soon became the name for Funakoshi's style of karate. Yoshitaka Funakoshi died in early 1945, his death from pneumonia probably precipitated by the news that his father's dojo had been destroyed in a bombing raid. After the war, Funakoshi returned to teaching in Tokyo, and in 1952, at the age of eighty-four, he undertook a three-month tour of American air bases, thus ensuring the spread of Shotokan karate to America. He died in 1957, the same year that the Japan Karate Association was founded and he was its first Chief Instructor. His memorial bears the words 'Karate ni sente nashi' – 'There is no first attack in karate'.

Ian MacLaren is the Karate Union of Great Britain Archive and Research Officer, he is recognised as one of the U.K.'s foremost Karate historians.

BREATHING –

The Essence of Karate

KIMÉ

Without breath there is no life. Without *Kimé* your Karate is lifeless.

It is essential that you understand that all Karate techniques must be performed with *Kimé*.

Kimé is the focusing of mental energy, breathing and physical force culminating in a single striking point.

Karate is not whole without all of these elements.

The key to *Kimé* is the breathing. Any physical activity requires correct breathing, which works with the body not against it. The grunts and groans athletes make are not for effect – they are using their breathing along with their muscles to explode with maximum effort, producing the most potent force possible. No effort is wasted.

There are various methods of breathing, but the basic method for beginners is: 'One Breath One Technique'.

In a relaxed but controlled manner breathe out through a slightly opened mouth, complete the breath and technique at the same moment closing your mouth instantly as if biting. Simultaneously tense the abdomen, locking the rest of your muscles for a fraction of a second before relaxing and breathing in normally.

As you tense and lock the muscles of the abdomen, the buttocks should be clenched so that the abdomen lifts up and forward.

Left: The body in a relaxed posture before performing a basic punch.

Right: The body on completion of the punch with *Kimé*.

POSTURE OF THE SPINE

The position of the spine is very important to the posture of a Karate technique and can effect the correct breathing method.

This is the normal posture of the spinal column in a standing position and should be maintained when in your basic stances.

This is done by tensing the muscles of the buttocks and lifting the pelvic curvature forward and up.

When performed incorrectly the discs of the lumbar curvature are compressed.

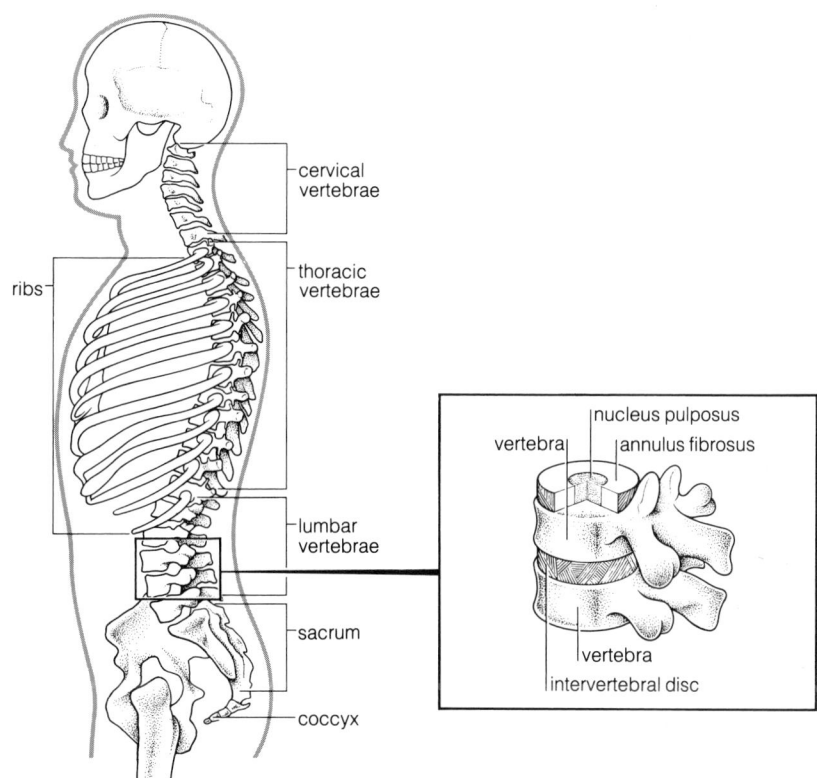

Left: This picture shows the incorrect posture when in front stance. Note the curvature of the lumbar region. This will cause lower back pain and techniques performed in this position will tend to lean forward.

Right: This picture shows the correct posture when in front stance.

KIAI
Spirit-meeting or energy-shout

The *Kiai* is the shout at the end of a technique and in conjunction with the expulsion of air (*Kimé*) will maximise the power of the movement. It also has the effect of surprising an opponent and may momentarily paralyse their response.

The concept of *Ki* is at the root of all martial arts and Japanese philosophy. *Ki* is the **spirit** and **energy** along with the breath **meeting** *Ai* at the moment of impact.

Developing your *Kiai* is very important. It is not just a shout or screech from the throat. If you put your hand on your stomach and cough you will feel the muscles of your abdomen contract. This in fact is the start of your *Kiai*.

First understand the principles and the breathing method *Kimé* as explained, then replace the biting action with your shout '*Kiai*'.

It will start as a growl from the pit of the stomach but when completed the sound produced will vary from one to another.

Points to avoid are:

- the mouth open too wide
- saying the word '*Kiai*'
- shouting without using the breathing method *Kimé*

KOSHI

Use of the Hips

KOSHI
Use of the Hips

The fundamental source of power in Karate is the hips. The use of thrusting and rotating movements of the hips harnessed to correct breathing produces a force that to the uninformed has appeared quite mystical. In reality it is simply good bio-mechanics, the correct use of technique and continued practice.

This position is *Hanmi* (hips half facing the front). Normally used for front hand jab punches and blocks.

The position of the hips here is 10° from being square and is the position used for front hand lunge punches.

Don't open the hips too much as this pulls the front knee across the body.

Hips in the lunge punch posture.

It is important when practising the hip movements that you rotate the hips in the correct way. Use the hip joint of the front leg as the axis, thrusting the rear hip joint forward. To use an analogy, the upper torso should be like a door closing with the hinges on the hip that is forward. It is a common mistake for students to use their upper torso like a rotating door which rotates around a central axis, in this case the spinal column.

This hip position is square to the front and used for reverse hand techniques.

Push strongly with the back leg and do not allow the heel to lift.

DACHI

Stances

It cannot be emphasised enough how important the basic stances are to your Karate practice.

They are the foundation of all techniques. A strong punch, kick or block is only effective if the stance and, even more important, how to move into the stance is understood.

A tree will not grow without strong roots and your Karate will not progress without good *Dachi*.

ZENKUTSU-DACHI
Front Stance

This is a strong stance and the one most used; it is especially effective when attacking but is also used for blocks and kicks.

The distance between the feet is approximately two shoulder widths long and one shoulder width wide with 60% of your body weight forward.

The hips should remain centred with your front knee pushed forward over your big toe; your back foot should point to the front with the knee locked.

The front foot should be turned slightly inward so you can use the full width of the foot when stepping.

Points to avoid are:

- stance too long
- stance too narrow
- back foot points out to the side
- the front knee too much to one side or the other
- heel of the rear foot raised

FORWARD

60% of your body weight should be on the front leg with the back foot and knee facing forward.

FORWARD

Keep your front knee forward in a line with the big toe, your weight centred and your front foot turned slightly in.

Push off the back leg, bending through the front knee to maintain the hips at the same height.

Stepping through with the back leg, 100% of the body weight should now be on the front leg.

Thrust forward with the hips and support leg, landing with the ball of the front foot first – not the heel – and end your breath.

STEPPING IN FRONT STANCE

Bring your knee through centre with 95% of your weight on the front leg. Ensure you do not lean forward.

Continue to step through centre with the back leg, your hips should now be above the support foot.

Thrust the hips and support leg forward ending the stance and your breath together.

ZENKUTSU-DACHI
Front Stance

← STEPPING IN FRONT STANCE

Thrust the leg back into the stance, locking the knee and ending your breath.

Bring the front leg through centre, pushing the hips back.

← STEPPING IN FRONT STANCE

Thrust the leg back into the stance, locking the knee and ending your breath.

Bring the front leg through centre, pushing the hips back.

Push back with the front leg, releasing the tension of the back leg knee to maintain the hips at the same height.

60% of your body weight should be on the front leg with the back foot and knee facing forward.

Push back with the front leg, releasing the tension of the back leg knee to maintain the hips at the same height.

Keep your front knee forward in a line with the big toe, your weight centred and your front foot turned slightly in.

KOKUTSU-DACHI
Back Stance

This stance is very effective when blocking at an angle. The weight on the back leg allows fast counter kicks off the front leg, or a powerful thrust off the back leg changing into front stance and delivering an

FORWARD

Points to avoid are:

- too much weight on the front leg
- hips open too much
- front knee drops inside the stance
- leaning forward with the upper body

70% of your weight on the back leg and hips at 45°. Both heels should be in line.

Push off the back leg, moving your weight forward.

FORWARD

70% of your body weight on the back leg and hips at 45°. Both heels should be in line.

Push off the back leg, keeping your hips the same height.

upper body counter-attack.

The distance between the feet is approximately two shoulder widths long with both heels in the same line.

70% of your body weight should be on the back leg with your hips at a 45° angle. The knee of the back leg should be bent and just inside the foot.

The front knee should be slightly bent with the weight on the ball of the foot.

STEPPING IN BACK STANCE

Continue moving forward, turning your hips to the front.

Push your back leg through, retaining all your weight on the support leg.

Pivot on the ball of the support foot, keeping 70% of your weight on the back leg.

STEPPING IN BACK STANCE

Square your hips and bring your back leg through centre.

Push your back leg forward, retaining all your weight on the support leg.

Pivot on the ball of the support foot, keeping 70% of your weight on the back leg and open your hips at a 45° angle.

KOKUTSU-DACHI
Back Stance

Complete the stance and end the breath together.	Continue to step back and start to open the hips.	Bring your front leg through centre with your hips to the front.

Complete the stance and end the breath together.	Continue to step back and start to open the hips.	Bring your front leg through centre keeping your knees close together.

Pushing off the front leg, pivot on the ball of the back foot.

Your stance should be approximately two shoulder widths long.

Pushing off the front leg, pivot on the ball of the back foot and square your hips.

70% of your body weight on the back leg and hips at 45°.

KIBA-DACHI
Straddle-leg Stance

FORWARD

This stance is very effective when blocking or attacking to the side and is sometimes referred to as Horse Stance because of the body posture.

The distance between the feet is approximately two shoulder widths long with both heels in the same line.

Fifty per cent of your body weight should be on each leg with your hips square.

Both feet should point forward with the knees pushed forward and outward.

Keep your buttocks flexed and abdomen lifted upward to prevent the upper body leaning forward.

Points to avoid are:

- stance too long or too short
- upper body leaning forward or backward
- too much weight on one or the other leg
- the buttocks relaxed and protruding to the rear

50% of your weight on each leg, feet forward and your heels in line with the hips square.

Stepping back in straddle-leg stance is exactly the same as stepping forward.

50% of your weight on each leg, feet forward and your heels in line with the hips square.

Push off the rear leg, keeping the hips the same height.

Bring your back foot across your front leg. Do not interfere with the support knee or over step.

Push down with the step over foot and out with the support leg into the stance.

With your heels in line push 60% of your weight on the front leg and keep your upper body straight.

Step across and keep your hips the same height with the balls of both feet in line.

Step out with the support leg ending the stance and breath together.

TSUKI

Punching

In general, punches (Tsuki) are thrusting arm movements delivered with the knuckles of the index and middle fingers (Seiken). The basic punches travel in a straight line – the shortest route from A to B – with the forearm rotating inward 180° as the punch is completed. The wrist must be kept tense with the back of the hand forming a straight line.

MAKING A FIST

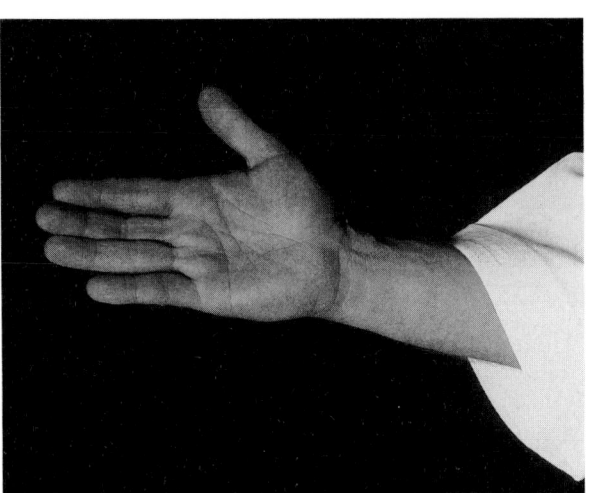

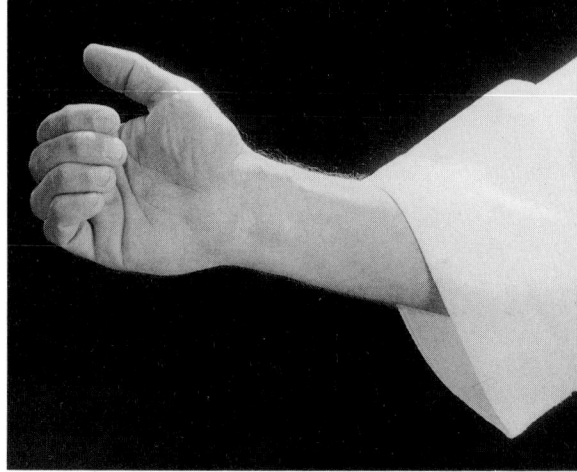

Start with your hand open and thumb out to the side.

Fold the fingers inward and curve the palm so that it forms a natural crease.

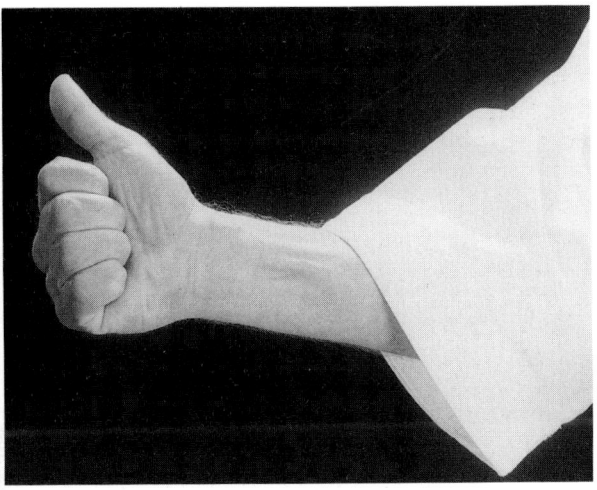

Put your finger tips tightly into the crease.

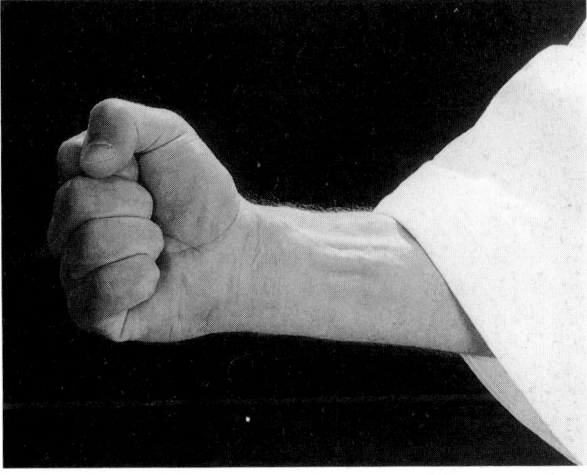

Bring your thumb across and press firmly against the index finger. Ensure you do not push across with the base joint of the thumb as this will disturb the index and middle fingers, causing them to protrude.

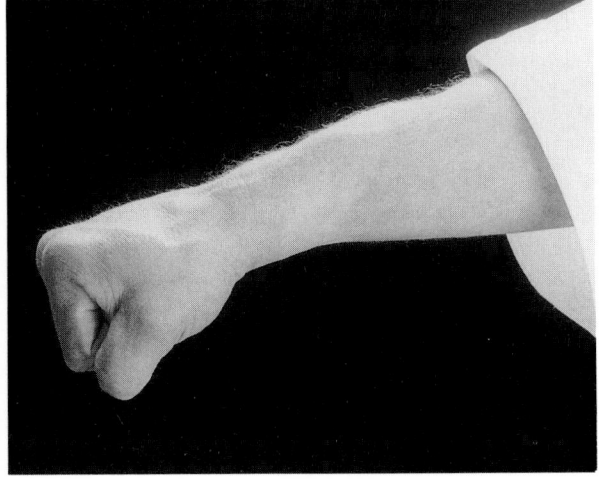

Once the fist is correctly made, the wrist should be tensed, with the top of the fist in line with the top of the forearm.

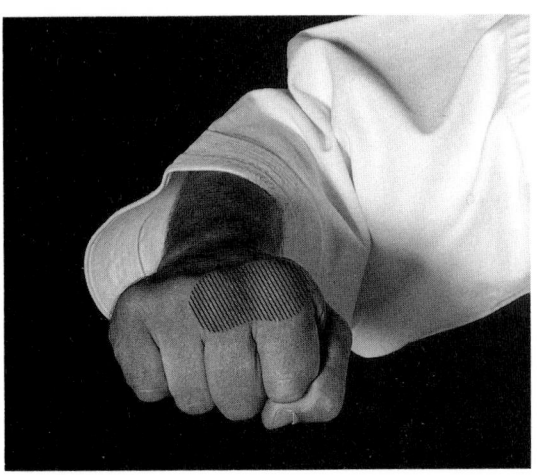

The part of the fist used when punching is the knuckles of the index and middle fingers.

CHOKU-ZUKI
Straight Punch

This basic arm movement promotes the correct path and performance of a punch while practising the breathing technique.

Ensure you do not twist the punching fist too soon as this could cause damage to the elbow joint.

Keep your hips and shoulders square and relaxed and slightly bend the knees so the stance is firm.

Start to push your attacking arm forward whilst retracting the other arm.

Punch to the centre and do not lift your shoulders. Keep both feet facing the front.

Twist the fist of the retracting arm, turning the elbow downward.

Continue both arm movements while breathing out.

Don't twist your attacking fist too soon.

Twist the fist completing the punch and breath together.

Keep your elbows close to your body.

Your retracting arm should be kept close to your body throughout the punch.

Ensure the elbow of the retracting arm is tight to the body and the punch is to the centre.

GYAKU-ZUKI
Reverse Punch

This powerful punch performed with the rotation of the hips, strong stance and explosive breathing, is mostly used to counter an opponent after blocking their attack.

Points to avoid are:

- over extending the punch and lifting the back heel
- pulling the front knee back to produce a negative hip action, when rotating the hips
- twisting the punching fist too soon, so that the arm snaps out from the elbow
- twisting the fist of the retracting arm too late so the path curves back to the side of the body

Start from a front stance with your forward arm out and hips at a 45° angle. Keep the elbow of the punching arm pulled back and tight to the body.

Start from a front stance with your forward arm out and hips at a 45° angle. Keep the elbow of the punching arm pulled back and tight to the body.

Start to rotate the hips and push your attacking arm forward whilst retracting the other arm.

Continue both arm movements without moving the front knee.

Thrust strongly from the back leg, twisting the hips and completing the punch and breath.

Twist the fist of the retracting arm, turning the elbow downward.

Keep your elbows close to your body and your hips level.

Ensure the elbow of the retracting arm is tight to the body and the punch is to the centre.

OI-ZUKI
Lunge Punch

This is the most powerful basic punch and is normally used as an attack.

The lungeing step using the full weight of the body, explosive arm movement and correct breathing produces devastating effects.

Points to avoid are:

- moving the front foot before you start to step
- any backward movement of the body before you move forward
- leaning forward with the upper torso
- punching too soon so the hip over-rotates, causing loss of balance
- landing, then punching – you must end both together

Starting from a front stance with your forward arm out and punching arm pulled back tight to the body.

Starting from a front stance with your forward arm out and punching arm pulled back tight to the body.

Move forward maintaining your hand and hip position.

Continue to step through without changing the hip and arm positions.

Pushing strongly with the back leg, thrust the hip forward, landing in a front stance and completing the punch; step and breath together.

Keep your weight centred and ensure you do not lean forward.

Keep the weight on the support leg and knees close together.

Punch to the centre and maintain a good front stance.

KIZAMI-ZUKI
Jab Punch

This punch is mostly used in conjunction with another punch or as a counter.

Points to avoid are:

- over-rotation of the hips
- leaning with the torso
- lifting the shoulders
- movement of the front knee

Starting in a reverse punch position.

Starting in a reverse punch position.

Start to push your attacking arm forward whilst retracting the other arm.

Continue both arm movements keeping your shoulders relaxed.

Sharply twist the hips to a 45° angle, completing the punch and breath together.

Twist the fist of the retracting arm, turning the elbow downward.

Keep your elbows close to your body and hips square.

Ensure the elbow of the retracting arm is tight to the body and the punch is to the centre.

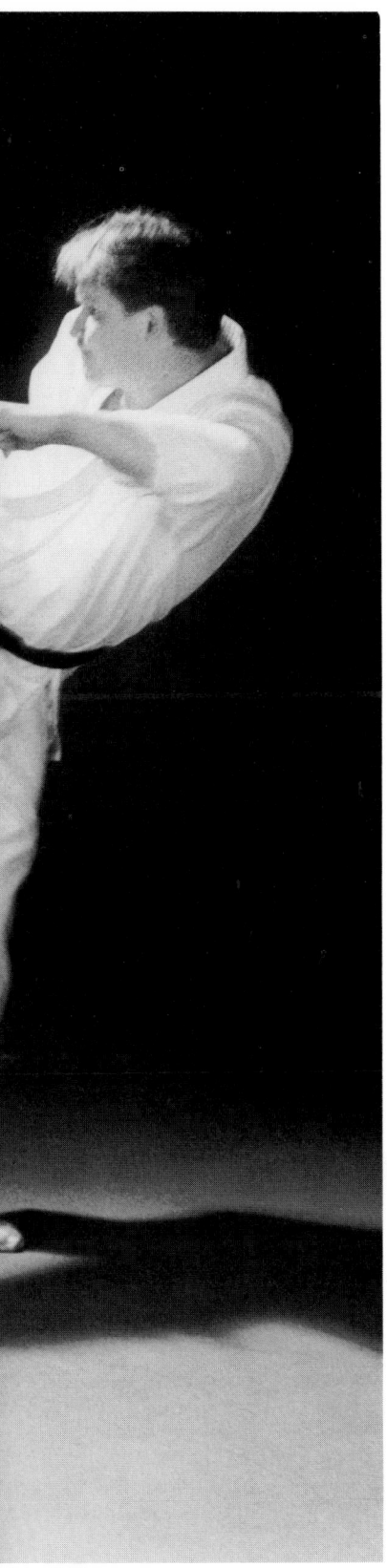

UKE

Blocking

Blocking (Uke) techniques make Karate unique amongst fighting systems; no other form of combat puts as much emphasis on defence using blocks. Most blocks use an arcing action to deflect attacks safely away from the target. The contact part of most blocks is the wrist, opening an opponent's body for a counter-attack.

AGE-UKE
Rising block

The Rising Block is an upper level defence against direct attacks to the face and downward attacks to the head.

Points to avoid are:

- lifting the shoulders
- obscuring the vision with the blocking arm
- over-rotation of the hips

Start with the hips at 45° and the retracting hand held high and open.

Turn the hips square and start to retract the raised arm.

Continue to retract the raised arm and bring the blocking arm across and in front.

The raised arm should be at a 45° angle with the opposite arm pulled back tight to the body.

Twist the wrist, turning the elbow in and downwards.

The blocking arm travels directly from your hip to this position.

Open the hips to 45° and pull the retracting arm back to the hip.
Twist the wrist of the blocking arm and raise above your head.

End the hip movement, retraction arm and the block together with your breath.

APPLICATION

As your opponent attacks with a straight punch to the face, step back making contact with his wrist and the wrist of your blocking arm.

Complete your defence by deflecting his arm upwards.

This picture demonstrates a method of checking that your blocking arm is the correct distance from your forehead, approximately a fist width.

SOTO-UKE
Outside Block

Points to avoid are:

- the blocking arm sweeping round too low and close to the body
- allowing the fist to precede the elbow

The Outside Block is predominately a middle level block sweeping across the body from outside inward making contact with the wrist.

Start with the hips at 45° and the retracting arm extended to the front. The blocking arm is raised and held behind the head.

Square your hips and twist the wrist of the retracting arm. The blocking arm is brought around the shoulder.

Continue the retraction of the arm and bring the blocking arm in front of the body.

The blocking arm elbow should be at shoulder height.

The blocking arm elbow is still shoulder height and the elbow of the retracting arm is now downward.

Keep the wrist and the elbow of the blocking arm in the same line.

- twisting the blocking arm wrist too soon
- over-rotation of the hips

As your opponent attacks with a straight punch to the body, step back making contact with his wrist and the wrist of your blocking arm.

Twist the hips to 45°, complete the retraction of the arm to the hip, and twist the wrist of the blocking arm sweeping it across the body.

Complete your defence by deflecting his arm across your body.

Showing outside block as a defence to a side thrust kick.

End the hip movement, retraction, block and breath together. Ensure the block covers the body with the fist at shoulder height.

This picture demonstrates a method of checking that your blocking arm is the correct distance from your body, approximately a fist width.

UCHI-UKE
Inside Block

The Inside Block is predominately a middle level block originating from the opposite hip, blocking across the body from inside outward, making contact with the wrist.

Points to avoid are:

- lifting the shoulders
- blocking arm too high in its preparation
- arm too close to the body when the block is completed
- early rotation of the hips

Start with the hips square and the retracting arm extended to the front. The blocking arm is across the body with your hand on the opposite hip.

Twist the wrist of the retracting arm and start to pull it back. Bring the blocking arm forward keeping the elbow low.

Keep the blocking arm close to the body with your elbow pointing forward.

Keep the shoulders down and the elbows inside the body line.

Twist the hips to 45°. Complete the retraction of the arm to the hip, and twist the wrist of the blocking arm bringing it across the body.

End the hip movement, retraction, block and breath together. Ensure the block covers the body with the fist at shoulder height.

APPLICATION

As your opponent attacks with a straight punch to the body, step back making contact with his wrist and the wrist of your blocking arm.

Complete your defence by deflecting his arm across your body.

Showing inside block as a defence to a roundhouse kick.

This picture demonstrates a method of checking that your blocking arm is the correct distance from your body, approximately a fist width.

SHUTO-UKE
Knife-hand Block

The Knife-hand Block is predominately a middle level block normally performed at an angle using back stance.

Points to avoid are:

- lifting the shoulders
- blocking arm elbow too high
- twisting the blocking arm wrist too early

Start with the hips square and the retracting arm extended to the front. The blocking arm is across the body and to the side of the head.

Twist the wrist of the retracting arm and start to pull it back. Bring the blocking arm forward keeping the elbow low.

Extend the blocking arm and start to turn the hips.

Keep your shoulders down and the blocking arm elbow close to the chest.

Keep your elbows inside your body line.

Keep the retracting arm tight to the body.

- blocking arm too straight
- over-rotation of the hips
- loss of balance

Twist the hips to 45°. Complete the retraction of the arm to the centre of the chest. Twist the wrist of the blocking arm bringing it across the body.

End the hip movement, retraction, block and breath together.
Ensure that the block covers the body with the knife-hand at shoulder height.

APPLICATION

As your opponent attacks with a straight punch to the body step back making contact with his wrist and the wrist of your blocking arm.

Complete your defence by deflecting his arm with a twist of your wrist, making a cutting action with the edge of your hand whilst landing in back stance at an angle.

This picture demonstrates a method of checking that your blocking arm is the correct distance from your body, approximately a fist width.

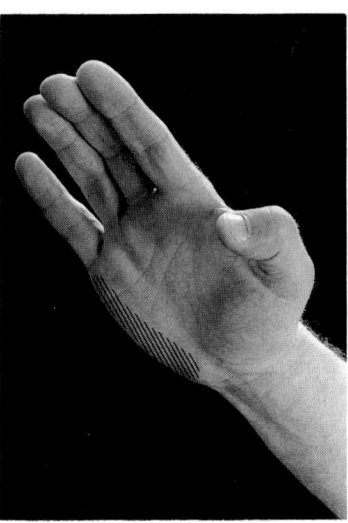

This picture shows the position of the knife-hand. The palm and the fingers should be stretched out and tensed, the first joint of the thumb should be bent with the back of the hand, wrist and forearm in line. Ensure you do not bend the base joint of the thumb, this will cause the palm to lose its tension.
The contact area is between the little finger and the wrist.

GEDAN-BARAI
Downward Block

The Downward Block is a lower level sweeping defence normally used against kicks and punches to the abdomen and groin.

Points to avoid are:

- lifting the shoulders
- leaning forward
- elbow of the blocking arm too high in its preparation
- blocking too far across the body
- over-rotating the hips

Start with the hips square and retracting arm extended to the front and downward. The blocking arm is across the body and to the side of the head.

Twist the wrist of the retracting arm and bring the blocking arm downward keeping the elbow low.

Keep the shoulders down and the blocking arm elbow close to the chest.

Keep the elbows inside the body line.

Twist the hips to 45°. Complete the retraction of the arm back to the hip and twist the wrist of the blocking arm, bringing it across the body.

End the hip movement, retraction, block and breath together. Ensure that the block covers the body.

APPLICATION

As your opponent attacks with a front kick to your abdomen, step back making contact with his ankle and the wrist of your blocking arm.

Complete your defence by deflecting his leg to the side.

KERI

Kicking

In Karate, kicking (Keri) techniques are the most spectacular and the most powerful. However, performing the kicks effectively requires a great amount of practice. Balance is difficult because the body weight is supported by one leg, and is even more difficult when the kick is completed as the shock on impact has to be absorbed and controlled.

When kicking, use the body especially the hips and not just the kicking leg. Withdraw the kick quickly to retain balance and prevent the opponent catching the leg.

MAE-GERI
Front Kick

The Front Kick is the most natural kick to perform and is generally the first taught.

The snap of the knee and forward thrust of the hips yields a powerful, quick and very effective kick.

As you deliver the front kick you must keep your shoulders relaxed to ensure good balance and flowing movement.

The lead hand should be forward until the kick is completed, and then changed as you land in the correct stance.

Keep your hips square during the kick with the support foot pointing forward.

Start in front stance. Hips in *Hanmi* (half facing the front).

Lift the knee up squaring your hips to the front.

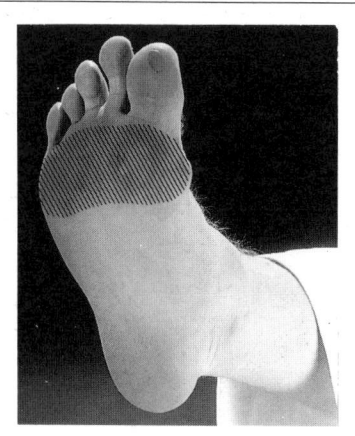

The contact area used is the ball of the foot.

Keep your weight firmly on the front leg.

Keep your support leg bent and your shoulders relaxed.

Snap your leg out pushing your hips into the kick. End the kick and breath together.

Snap the leg back retaining balance and posture.

Use the support leg to push firmly into front stance.

Kick to the centre of your body with the toes pulled back, hitting with the ball of the foot.

Keep your knee up and hips square.

Change your hips and hands to *Hanmi* (half facing the front).

YOKO-GERI-KEAGE
Side Snap Kick

This is a kick used at close range to vulnerable areas of the body, such as groin, knee and arm joints, ribs and throat.

It is performed with a fast curving snap from the knee.

Again you must have relaxed shoulders for effective delivery. The hip should lift and retract sharply as the leg is snapped out and returned. Remember the hip lifts, it does not rotate, otherwise the path of the kick will alter.

It is important to ensure the knee of the kicking leg always points towards the target.

Start in a straddle-leg stance with the head and hands to the side.

Step across, keeping the hips the same height.

Transfer your weight to the support leg and turn your hips a little towards the target, lifting your knee.

Keep your arms either side of your body throughout the kick.

Don't allow the step over leg to interfere with the support knee.

Keep your support leg bent, point your knee to the target and keep your raised foot close to your support leg.

The contact area used is the upper edge of the foot.

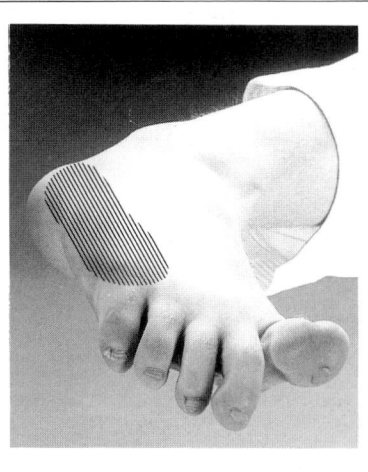

Snap the leg out from the knee in an upward curving action, lifting the hip.

Immediately snap the leg and hip back, keeping the knee the same height.

Push down firmly into straddle-leg stance.

End the kick and the breath at the same time.

Maintain posture and balance.

End the stance and another breath together.

YOKO-GERI-KEKOMI
Side Thrust Kick

This is a very powerful kick when performed correctly. It is slower than the Front and Roundhouse kicks, so it is mainly used in a defensive manner to stifle an oncoming attack.

You must fully commit your hips and body weight into the kick otherwise you could 'bounce' off your target, losing balance and momentum.

Start in a straddle-leg stance with the head and hands to the side.

Step across keeping the hips the same height.

Thrust the hips and leg out to the side.

Immediately withdraw the leg, keeping the knee high.

Transfer your weight to the support leg and lift your knee.

Pivot on the support foot, opening the hips so the kicking leg lifts at the ankle.

Push down firmly into straddle-leg stance.

YOKO-GERI-KEKOMI
Side Thrust Kick

Keep your arms either side of your body throughout the kick.

Don't allow the step over leg to interfere with the support knee.

End the kick and the breath at the same time locking the leg.

Maintain posture and balance.

Keep your support leg bent and your shoulders relaxed.

Keep the knee the same height with your head, shoulders and arms still.

The contact area used is the outside edge of the foot.

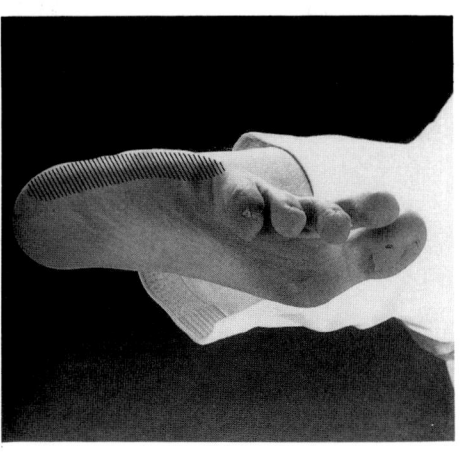

End the stance and another breath on landing.

MAWASHI-GERI
Roundhouse Kick

The Roundhouse Kick is one of the most spectacular kicks in Karate. Timed to perfection it is very difficult to defend against with the rotation of the hips producing considerable power.

However, if this technique is not executed correctly you are at risk of injury to the knee and lower back, and groin strains.

You are also open to an opponent's counter-attack as your balance will be vulnerable and defence limited.

Start in front stance with hips in *Hanmi* (half facing the front).

Lift the knee up to the side, keeping your hips and upper body still.

Pivot on the ball of the support foot, rotating the hips and upper body.

Keep your weight firmly on your front leg.

Be careful not to bring the knee in front of the hip joint.

Keep the shoulder and arm of the kicking leg outside of the kick.

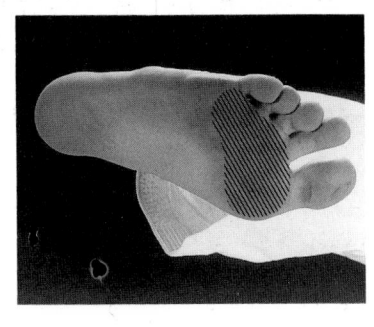

The contact area used is the ball of the foot.

As the pivot is completed snap the leg out from the knee.

Snap the kick back from the knee joint.

Pivot on the support foot, rotating the hips forward into front stance.

Keep the support foot flat on the floor, ending the hip movement, kick and breath together.

Retain your balance and posture.

End the stance and another breath together.

USHIRO-GERI
Back Kick

This is the most powerful of the basic kicks. The 180° pivot and backward thrust of the hips will produce a strong attack.

However, balance is difficult due to the turn involved and the back will be exposed, making defence difficult.

Start in front stance with hips in *Hanmi* (half facing the front).

Pivot on the front foot, turning the hips and support leg.

Square the hips and lift the kicking leg.

Keep your weight firmly on the front leg.

Keep looking forward with your hands in a ready posture.

Look straight in front at this point so that you do not over-rotate the hips.

The contact area used is the heel of the foot.

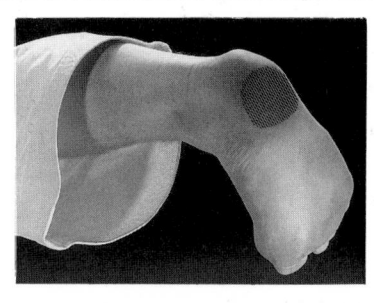

Thrust the leg out, pushing your hips back and locking the knee.

Quickly look over your shoulder as you withdraw the kicking leg.

Pivot again on the support foot, rotating your hips and land firmly into front stance.

End the kick and the breath together.

Bring your arms round rotating your upper body.

End the stance and another breath together.

UCHI

Striking

Striking (Uchi) techniques use a snapping action of the arm with the elbow as the main pivot. The shoulders are also used to some extent and are the main source of power when striking with the elbow.

The snapping action when using the back fist (Uraken) or knife hand (Shuto) should be relaxed with the forearm making an arc-like path to the target. Striking techniques are primarily used as a counter-attack or to follow up an initial punch or kick.

SHUTO-UCHI *Knife-hand Strike*
NUKITE-UCHI *Spear-hand*

A combination of strikes are shown here using the Knife- and Spear-hand.

Start in the front stance with hips at 45°.

Start to step forward and lift the striking hand up to the side of the head with your elbow and shoulders in line.

Continue the sequence by bringing the striking arm back to the opposite shoulder and square the hips to the front.

Open the hips and strike out with the knife-hand across the body, completing another breath.

Continue to step forward and square the hips to the front.

Rotate the hips and bring the striking hand forward and across the body. The opposite arm is retracted to the hip. Complete the stance, breath and strike together.

Continue the sequence by retracting the striking arm back to the hips whilst rotating the hips forward and strike with the spear-hand. Complete with another breath.

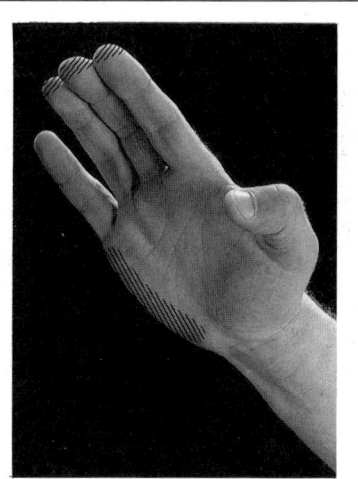

Contact areas for knife-hand strike (side of hand) and spear-hand (tips of fingers)

SHUTO-UCHI *Knife-hand Strike*
NUKITE-UCHI *Spear-hand*

Start in a front stance with hips at 45°.

Start to step forward, lifting the front arm up with hand open whilst raising the striking hand up to the side of the head.

Bring the striking arm back from the elbow joint and rotate the hand whilst squaring the hips to the front.

Open the hips and strike out with the knife-hand across the body.

Continue to step forward and square the hips, keeping the striking arm back.

Complete the strike and ensure the hand is across the body with the elbow slightly bent.

Continue the sequence by retracting the striking arm and rotate the hips forward and strike with the spear-hand. Make sure the strike is to the centre.

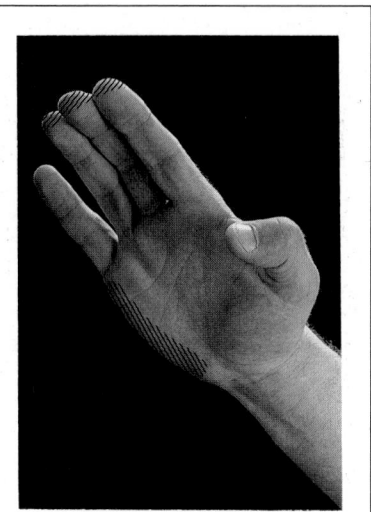

Contact areas for knife-hand strike (side of hand) and spear-hand (tips of fingers)

URAKEN-UCHI
Back-fist Strike

Start in a front stance with hips at 45°.

Start to step forward, square the hips and bring the striking fist to the opposite shoulder.

Continue to step forward, keeping the hips square.

Start in a front stance with hips at 45°.

Start to step forward, square the hips and bring the striking fist across to the opposite shoulder.

Continue to step forward, keeping the hips square.

Open the hips and snap the arm out from the elbow, striking with the back of the fist. Instantly retract the arm keeping the elbow still. Complete the stance, breath and strike together.

Open the hips and snap the arm out across the body, striking with the back of the fist. Instantly retract the arm, keeping the elbow still. Complete the stance, breath and strike together.

Contact area for Uraken is the back of the hand.

EMPI-UCHI
Elbow Strike

Using a straddle-leg stance bring your striking arm across the body and the retracting arm forward.

Complete the strike by thrusting the elbow to the side and retract the other arm to the hip. End the strike and breath together.

Ensure the striking arm is across the body but not too close to the chest.

Complete the strike by thrusting the elbow in a direct line to the target. End the strike and breath together.

Note: By keeping the striking arm away from the body you will ensure your elbow does not travel in a circular action.

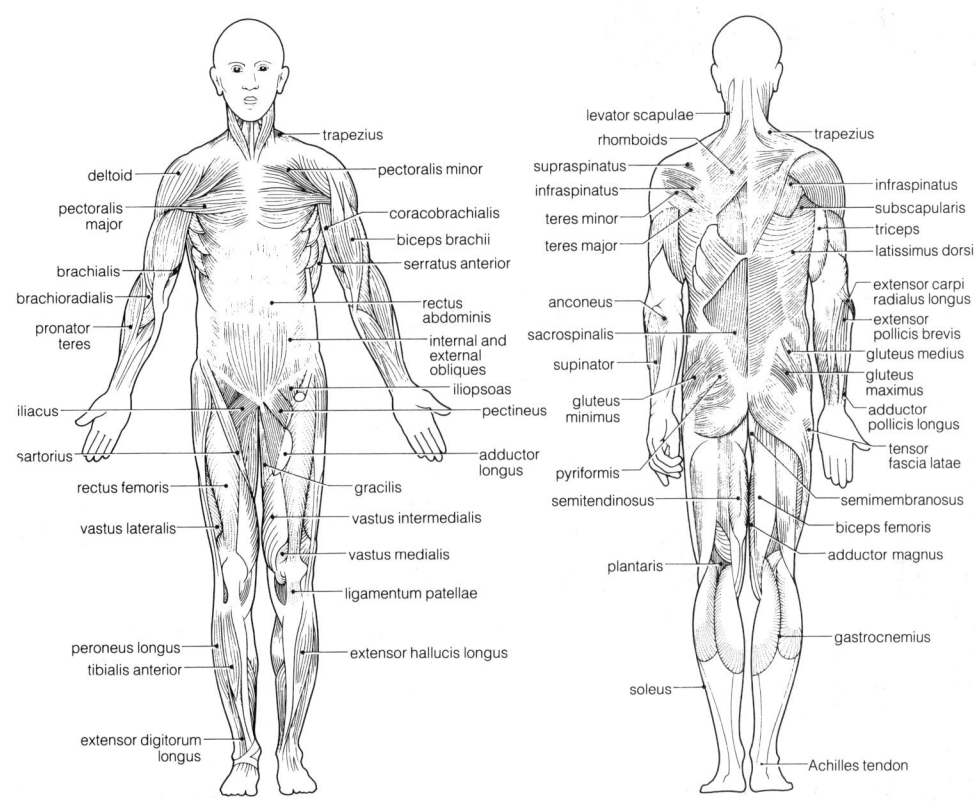

Muscle System

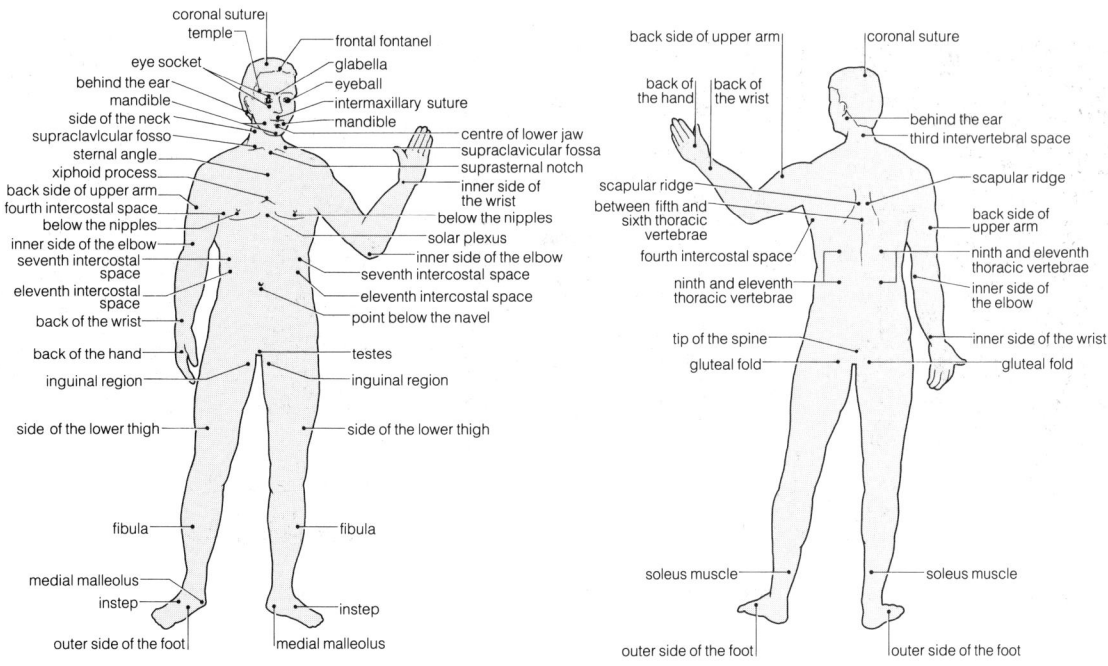

Vulnerable Points of the Body

Glossary

Age-Uke (Ah-Geh Oo-Kay) Rising block
Choku-Zuki (Cho-Koo Zoo-Key) Straight punch
Chudan (Chew-Dahn) Chest area
Dachi (Dah-Chee) Stance
Dojo (Dough-Joe) Training hall
Empi-Uchi (Em-Pee Oo-Chee) Elbow strike
Gedan (Geh-Dahn) Lower area of the body
Gedan-Barai (Geh-Dahn Baa-Rah-Ee)
Downward block
Gyaku-Zuki (Gya-Koo Zoo-Key) Reverse punch
Hanmi (Hahn-Me) Half front facing position
Jodan (Joe-Dahn) Face area
Karate (Kah-Rah-Teh) Empty hand
Keage (Kay-Ah-Geh) Snap kick
Kekomi (Kay-Koh-Me) Thrust kick
Keri (Kay-Rhee) Kicking
Kiai (Key-Eye) Spirit meeting or energy shout
Kiba-Dachi (Kay-Bah Dah-Chee) Straddle-leg
stance
Kimé (Key-May) Focusing mental and physical
force
Kizami-Zuki (Key-Zah-Me Zoo-Key) Jab punch
Kokutsu-Dachi (Koe-Koo-Tsu Dah-Chee) Back
stance
Koshi (Go-She) Use of the hips

Koshi (Ko-She) Ball of the foot
Mae-Geri (Mah-eh Geh-Rhee) Front kick
Mawashi-Geri (Mah-Wha-She Geh-Rhee)
Roundhouse kick
Nukite (Noo-Key-Teh) Spear hand
Oi-Zuki (Oh-Ee-Zoo-Key) Lunge punch
Seiken (See-Ken) Fore fist
Shuto-Uchi (Shoe-Toe Oo-Chee) Knife-hand
strike
Shuto-Uke (Shoe-Toe Oo-Kay) Knife-hand block
Sokuto (Sow-Koo-Toe) Edge of the foot
Soto-Uke (So-Toh Oo-Kay) Outside block
Tsuki (Tsue-Key) Punching
Uchi (Oo-Chee) Striking
Uchi-Uke (Oo-Chee Oo-Kay) Inside block
Uke (Oo-Kay) Blocking
Uraken-Uchi (Oo-Rah-Ken Oo-Chee) Back-fist
strike
Ushiro-Geri (Oo-She-Row Geh-Rhee) Back kick
Yoko-Geri-Keage (Yoh-Koh Geh-Rhee Kay-Ah-
Geh) Side snap kick
Yoko-Geri-Kekomi (Yoh-Koh Geh-Rhee Kay-
Koh-Me) Side thrust kick
Zenkutsu-Dachi (Zen-Kou-Tsue Dah-Chee) Front
stance